These questions are answered by:

____

____

____

All your answers are not wrong
All your answers are not always right
All come from your bright or dark thoughts
All come truly, deeply from your heart and soul
And all come to define who you are at this very moment

DAY 1

If you could be a superhero who would you be and why?

DAY 2

What kind of workout has you always wanted to try? How hard will it be?

DAY 3

What is one thing you dislike the most about your job?

DAY 4

Pretend you are a raindrop falling to earth, describe your fall from the clouds.

DAY 5

List of things that have helped you through

DAY 6

What was the worst/weirdest haircut you have ever had?

DAY 7

Say something about your favorite movie.

DAY 8

Why do you not understand?

DAY 9

How do you deal with all the pressure of being on the same page?

DAY 10

If you could do it again, would you? Why?

DAY 11

Who are you going to look up to?

DAY 12

List of things that are important for happy families of all ages

DAY 13

What makes you want to be changed?

DAY 14

How would you describe the feeling of being isolated from people?

DAY 15

How would you describe your own personality?

DAY 16

How many times did you have to suck up your pride and ask for help?

DAY 17

What makes you question what you thought was valuable?

DAY 18

What is special about you? Explain what makes you a unique individual.

DAY 19

What's your next goal?

DAY 20

How old is the oldest pair of shoes in your closet?

DAY 21

What's your secret weapon?

DAY 22

Are you satisfied with what the day has been like? Why or why not?

DAY 23

What do you do when you want to have a little fun?

DAY 24

What is the one book you would still want to give to people who have never read it?

DAY 25

How do you deal with any kind of personal damage that you might get?

DAY 26

Why do you think of yourself as a person without 'privilege'?

DAY 27

How does your child feel when she's afraid?

DAY 28

What is the best way for you to attain happiness?

DAY 29

What is the best thing you remember doing?

DAY 30

If you could have one person tell you something different about yourself, what would you want them to say?

DAY 31

What is your favorite childhood activity?

DAY 32

How different was your life one year ago?

DAY 33

Would you rather the sun sets over the river and you eat strawberries all day or would you rather the stars are all the same color and you get to eat strawberries all day?

DAY 34

If you could put all of your fear and anxiety behind you, and all your frustration and disappointment behind you, what would you be?

DAY 35

What do you do when you're sure that your idea is at least somewhat right but it still needs some fine-tuning?

DAY 36

What's the best way for a person to lose weight?

DAY 37

What can you live for?

DAY 38

Do you get along with friends and family? Why?

DAY 39

What is the one thing you've come to regret the most in your life in the last ten years?

DAY 40

Describe a time when you became ill and missed out on doing something you'd really been looking forward to.

DAY 41

Say something about the life of an important person.

DAY 42

If you had to choose one thing to be honest, what would it be?

DAY 43

He saw her and he knew... [continue the sentence]

DAY 44

How will you suggest a process or method of innovating that will avoid clashing with existing systems?

DAY 45

If you had to choose one thing about how you are making your living, what would it be?

DAY 46

If you could go back a month, a week, a day? What would you do differently?

DAY 47

If you could be anything you wanted to be, what would it be?

DAY 48

Why do you think you've got the skill?

DAY 49

What's the best thing about being with a friend? Why are some friends better than others?

DAY 50

Is the most important purpose in life happiness? If not, what is?

DAY 51

What is one thing you think you would make better in the future?

DAY 52

Why do you have this weird attitude?

DAY 53

What's your first reaction when you are called 'a liar'?

DAY 54

List of things that you sell

DAY 55

List of things that have come up

DAY 56

How do you deal with the situation?

DAY 57

What does your favorite person say when you give him your attention?

DAY 58

What's a body part that you wouldn't mind losing?

DAY 59

What was (will be) the first thing that you did (do) when you got your driver's license?

DAY 60

Why does stupidity happen?

DAY 61

What is the most important thing you learned in school?

DAY 62

What's the worst thing that might happen?

DAY 63

If you could do anything and have nothing to lose for once in your wildest imagination, what would it be?

DAY 64

When was the last time you went to the movies alone?

DAY 65

If you had to choose to see a single scene that defined you from day one, what would it be?

DAY 66

What are you reading? Who's your favorite author?

DAY 67

What's your biggest disappointment in life?

DAY 68

What do you think about when you get drunk?

DAY 69

What can you tell someone with whom you don't belong?

DAY 70

What is something you never thought you could tell me but maybe want to tell me now?

DAY 71

What is the one thing that you would like to change or improve your business?

DAY 72

What are the words you use every day?

DAY 73

The air has no colors, he said. But why do I... (continue the sentence)

DAY 74

What causes you to feel the need to be an entrepreneur?

DAY 75

What have you done to convince yourself you will be a better person?

DAY 76

Would you rather be among the first? Why?

DAY 77

Why do you even want to know?

DAY 78

What would you like people to know about you?

DAY 79

What are your favorite shapes?

DAY 80

Would you rather use your power or not? Why?

DAY 81

Say something about your own life that you're not proud of.

DAY 82

What do you tell yourself when you want to believe the worst about people?

DAY 83

What are your deciding factors?

DAY 84

What do you have that you're not allowed to tell anyone?

DAY 85

Would you rather have an apple or a banana? Or perhaps you would rather be thrown into space?

DAY 86

What do you think your greatest strength is?

DAY 87

If you could teach someone how to sing, would you and why?

DAY 88

What do you hope for in this new life?

DAY 89

List of things that have been rejected

DAY 90

Imagine you're stuck on the roof of a house that has been carried away by a flood, which person would you most like to be on the roof with you?

DAY 91

When was the last time you felt confident?

DAY 92

Who do you think hates you right now?

DAY 93

List of books to read before you go to sleep

DAY 94

Are you confrontational? Why? Why not?

DAY 95

What is wrong with this picture?

DAY 96

How would you describe the feeling of being exhausted right now?

DAY 97

Where would you want to live if Earth was uninhabitable?

DAY 98

Who is your favorite celebrity? Why?

DAY 99

Would you rather it was a little more expensive or a little less expensive?

DAY 100

List the pros and cons of becoming immortal.

DAY 101

Why do you always say you need to be more consistent?

DAY 102

Are there any activities that you are teaching your kids that aren't good for them? What are those?

DAY 103

What is one thing you didn't learn today?

DAY 104

If you could stay in only one place, where would it be?

DAY 105

If you had to choose one thing that you believe that you have to do today to have the perfect day, what would that be?

DAY 106

What is the most important thing you want to do with your life?

DAY 107

What have you given so much to the other person? Will you limit it now?

DAY 108

What's the one thing you like to do every day?

DAY 109

Would you rather not have friends? Why?

DAY 110

Why would you leave your life at home for a night of partying?

DAY 111

List of things that made this purchase

DAY 112

What is most important to you to live your life the way you want?

DAY 113

When was the last time you felt like your life mattered?

DAY 114

How does a person get their dream job?

DAY 115

What is your favorite book?

DAY 116

What is one statement that you hope people will say about you after you die?

DAY 117

What is the one thing that doesn't make you cringe?

DAY 118

Would you rather be surrounded by people of differing opinions or surrounded by people who are all for equality?

DAY 119

How would you describe the feeling of being creative?

DAY 120

How would you describe the feeling of being somebody that's impossible to define?

DAY 121

What would it take to get you to stop talking about it?

DAY 122

What is one thing you are excited to see as soon as possible?

DAY 123

How do you deal with people who think they're superior?

DAY 124

What would you do if someone did something wrong?

DAY 125

What causes you to have that smile on your face?

DAY 126

How can you make things right with your life?

DAY 127

If you were a food, what would you be?

DAY 128

What is your opinion of D movies?

DAY 129

What do you do when there is no direction in your life?

DAY 130

What should you take away from this discussion?

DAY 131

Describe how weather affects your commute to school.

DAY 132

How do you deal with people who think as you do?

DAY 133

What's the favorite piece of advice you've found?

DAY 134

How can you prove you love another person?

DAY 135

Who was one of your best, or worst, teachers? Describe them.

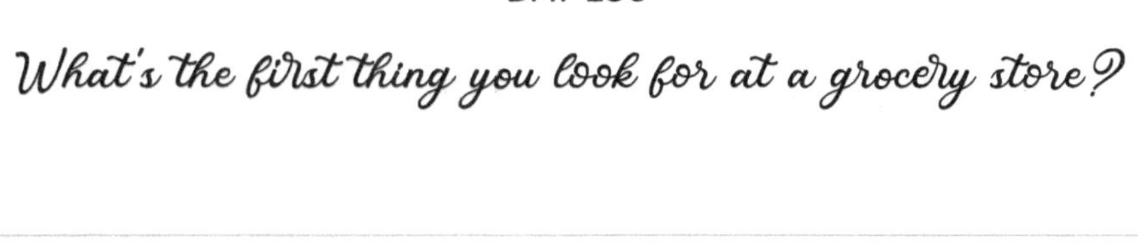

DAY 136

What's the first thing you look for at a grocery store?

DAY 137

What are some of your favorite hangovers?

DAY 138

What is most important to you at this moment today?

DAY 139

What do your kids look for in education?

DAY 140

Tell a story about yourself.

DAY 141

What's one thing about yourself you'd like to change?

DAY 142

What do you consume before bed each day?

DAY 143

Is it important to know your weaknesses? Why or why not?

DAY 144

What is your favorite piece of fiction that you have read and why?

DAY 145

If you could go back in time to the day you were born, what would you want to do?

DAY 146

Tell about your favorite vacation experience.

DAY 147

What would you do if you were living in an environment where nobody could speak?

DAY 148

What is the most significant brand you have owned?

DAY 149

If you were to die today, what would like people to say about you?

DAY 150

What would you do if you knew that every minute of every hour was the result of your actions and decisions?

DAY 151

Make a list of your favorite attributes.

DAY 152

How do you deal with people with no interest?

DAY 153

What is the one thing that you're sure about yourself?

DAY 154

What kind of people do you like?

DAY 155

What causes you to become emotionally attached to a person?

DAY 156

Which movie would you recommend if they were a great filmmaker?

DAY 157

What is the one thing that you regret most about growing up?

DAY 158

How do you deal with the fact that people might be saying something and you're going to want to do something?

DAY 159

What is your worst moment?

DAY 160

What's so horrible about the world that you just want to let it go and go away?

DAY 161

What would you say to people who told you that you couldn't do something?

DAY 162

If you had to choose one thing that made a big impact on your life, what would it be and why?

DAY 163

What is the most important for you to know?

DAY 164

Would you rather not see it?

DAY 165

If you had to choose one thing as an enemy, what would it be?

DAY 166

Do you fear death? Why?

DAY 167

What is your favorite combat technique?

DAY 168

What's your favorite type of music?

DAY 169

Did you ever have any "What if" stories? What are those?

DAY 170

What can you do to improve your team's ability to make the right plays?

DAY 171

Does time change from one day to the next and is this why some days seem to go on forever? Why?

DAY 172

What are three things you'd love to find out about?

DAY 173

What is one thing you have in common with your worst game character?

DAY 174

List of things that are guaranteed to not happen

DAY 175

What would you do if you could go back in time and do anything?

DAY 176

Tell about a time that you gave in to peer pressure.

DAY 177

What can you learn from others?

DAY 178

List of things that you will not take

DAY 179

What are you wearing now?

DAY 180

What are the best dares to say in truth or dare?

DAY 181

What does your biggest dream look like?

DAY 182

If you could have a one-on-one conversation in one hour, who would it be?

DAY 183

What would you say to someone who told you they loved you?

DAY 184

How do you tell if someone is lying?

DAY 185

Who do you respect the most?

DAY 186

What's worth spending more on getting the best?

DAY 187

What are you embarrassed about?

DAY 188

What have you always wanted to get for your birthday?

DAY 189

Why do you find yourself unable to do these things?

DAY 190

Do you think you are capable of handling a relationship right now? Why?

DAY 191

How do you deal with a person who hates you so much that it drives you crazy?

DAY 192

Would you rather have an odd job or one with greater security and benefits? Why?

DAY 193

What event would you rather die than live through?

DAY 194

What's the first thing you'll buy that you never bought before?

DAY 195

What's the funniest thing you've done?

DAY 196

What would you do to change the country and the world for the better if you were elected president?

DAY 197

What did you do today that you're not proud of?

DAY 198

If you could do whatever you wanted to right now, what would you do?

DAY 199

If you could change anything in the world, what would you change and how?

DAY 200

Would you rather hike a mountain or go to the beach?

DAY 201

List of things that I do to make other people happy

DAY 202

Why do you think you're so special?

DAY 203

How would you describe the feeling of being a bit of a side-show like that joke, might be funny but has some amount of pushback?

DAY 204

If you had to choose to change your name, which name would you choose and why?

DAY 205

Would you rather do the wrong thing and pay the penalty or rather do the right thing and feel miserable?

DAY 206

Would you rather be happy or angry? Why?

DAY 207

How do you deal with an enemy that is so confident in their strength?

DAY 208

What is the one thing you most want to change about yourself today?

DAY 209

Who do you admire the most?

DAY 210

What is the worst thing about a video game that you have never played?

DAY 211

Do you stand by your decisions? Why?

DAY 212

Why are we speaking in the third person?

DAY 213

What was one thing you were scared to do?

DAY 214

What is one thing that you could learn from the past and apply it to your future?

DAY 215

How would you describe yourself in three words?

DAY 216

If you could change anything about your past, what would it be?

DAY 217

Do you think that if you try to fix what's broken in yourself, you'll ever be able to get yourself to feel more and more? Why?

DAY 218

If you had to choose one thing to take away from your time on the planet, what would it be?

DAY 219

If you could be in any film, why would you choose it?

DAY 220

How do you cope when you get home late?

DAY 221

What's the thing you're feeling the most?

DAY 222

Do you prefer the freedom to have fun or the responsibility to live a certain life? Why?

DAY 223

What causes you discomfort in the bedroom?

DAY 224

Do you like to cook? Why?

DAY 225

How do you deal with the constant pressure of being in the midst of it?

DAY 226

How do you deal with any of the crazy questions?

DAY 227

What can you do to help you be more open by helping others in your life?

DAY 228

Where does your happiness come from?

DAY 229

What do you look forward to the most from this trip?

DAY 230

What's an average day like for you?

DAY 231

Tell a friend how you're doing. How do you say it?

DAY 232

What are you missing?

DAY 233

What's the single loudest sound you can make?

DAY 234

When you meet someone you haven't seen in a long time, you are often surprised by how much they have changed. Describe a time when this happened to you.

DAY 235

What is the one thing you wish you had more time for?

DAY 236

What did you do before you started this?

DAY 237

Would you rather take a gamble or take a nap?

DAY 238

List of things that you've heard that might have helped you along the way.

DAY 239

Does it bother you to be around someone who has bad manners? Why?

DAY 240

Would you rather be an insect or a bird?

DAY 241

Tell me about your state of mind now.

DAY 242

Talk about the things that turn you on

DAY 243

What are you working on right now?

DAY 244

Would you rather get something you did not put in or something you did not want? Why?

DAY 245

If you had to choose, what was your favorite worst moment?

DAY 246

How would you describe the feeling of being a baby?

DAY 247

What is the one thing you don't know about the way you thought about consciousness?

DAY 248

Why do you still believe people would go to war if you said so?

DAY 249

What is the one thing you miss about someone who has raised you that makes you cling to them?

DAY 250

List of things that might be worth more

DAY 251

What if you're given a time turner? What would you use it for?

DAY 252

What has been the best lesson you have learned?

DAY 253

If you had to choose just one thing to be given, what would it be?

DAY 254

Write about 9 things that make you feel lucky.

DAY 255

List of things that went wrong

DAY 256

What do you do if someone is just staring at you?

DAY 257

What is the one thing you've learned from all of this?

DAY 258

What is a true friend's greatest strength?

DAY 259

What is something so important that hate? Why?

DAY 260

What does 'happiness' mean to you?

DAY 261

What is a true lover like?

DAY 262

List of things to do before to actually get started

DAY 263

What are your parents' expectations about your future?

DAY 264

What is the best way to get girls to do things?

DAY 265

What makes it great to work?

DAY 266

If someone were to meet you for the first time, what would they think?

DAY 267

Are you working to figure out what has worked for others? Why?

DAY 268

What were the last words you exchanged?

DAY 269

If you had no money, what would you do?

DAY 270

What's your first reaction when you learn that there's an entire subculture devoted to your personal hobby?

DAY 271

What is a secret about you?

DAY 272

What are your biggest and proudest achievements to date?

DAY 273

If you were on a deserted island for one day, what would you do?

DAY 274

How do you deal with anxiety when you're not trying to deal with it?

DAY 275

Why do you think your hair is so fine?

DAY 276

Would you rather do a thing or a million things together or separately?

DAY 277

What is the one thing you say to see how they respond?

DAY 278

What was your most rewarding experience?

DAY 279

What is the one thing that can make or break your relationship?

DAY 280

In what ways have you felt yourself being empty?

DAY 281

What's the biggest misconception you think people have about you?

DAY 282

What is one thing you have in common with the person whom you met a while ago?

DAY 283

When was the last time you felt that sense of calmness and safety?

DAY 284

What does it mean to be happy?

DAY 285

Say something about how you were a nice guy/girl

DAY 286

How would you describe the feeling of being pure energy?

DAY 287

What do you find attractive in a stranger?

DAY 288

Why would you rather spend your hard-earned money on a computer than spend the money on food and a place to sleep?

DAY 289

Say something that makes you feel weird

DAY 290

What's something you do when you're alone that makes you feel safe?

DAY 291

When was the last time someone was nice to you?

DAY 292

In what ways happiness is necessary for you?

DAY 293

How do feel about what happened?

DAY 294

How would you describe the feeling of being independent?

DAY 295

How do you deal with failure?

DAY 296

What makes you think we would look at that situation differently?

DAY 297

If all your clothes could only be one color, what color would you choose and why?

DAY 298

What is one thing that you don't have to pay for but is expensive?

DAY 299

If you could make one item disappear from your world, what would it be?

DAY 300

Say something about the smell of you

DAY 301

What is your opinion of having set rules for people to follow?

DAY 302

What is the one thing you can't do? Why?

DAY 303

What is the most significant truth in your life?

DAY 304

List of things that you want to do that you've tried and now you regret

DAY 305

If you could only choose one of the five most dangerous countries to tour as a tourist, which country would it be?

DAY 306

What do you hope to see during the trip?

DAY 307

How do you deal with the constant pressure of wanting to meet people with similar interests or beliefs, especially at this young age?

DAY 308

What is the one thing that you're not happy with?

DAY 309

Is there a specific type of follower that you will not follow?

DAY 310

Consider some of the parents others had growing up, what type of person would you be if you had those situations?

DAY 311

What is one thing you as a music fan cannot live without?

DAY 312

What's your least favorite thing?

DAY 313

What makes someone want to be your friend or your lover?

DAY 314

What is most important to you and how did you get it?

DAY 315

Why do you use the word "cute"?

DAY 316

What two questions would you ask to get the most information about who a person truly is?

DAY 317

What is most important: self-respect, character or fitness?

DAY 318

What's your most annoying thing?

DAY 319

Tell about an article or book you read recently.

DAY 320

If you could have done anything differently in your life, what would it be?

DAY 321

Say something about your past and your future

DAY 322

If you could use one thing from one moment of your life to help others, what would you use?

DAY 323

If you could ask anyone one question, what would it be?

DAY 324

When you got here, did you feel like you already knew this place? Like you knew exactly where everything was?

DAY 325

What would the world be like if it was filled with male and female copies of you?

DAY 326

Favorite movie set in the '70s?

DAY 327

Who are your biggest inspirations?

DAY 328

What is your biggest thing you want your child to have?

DAY 329

If you had to use only one word to describe someone, what would it be?

DAY 330

Who could you turn to in times of sadness?

DAY 331

Say something about our relationship to the world that resonates with you.

DAY 332

What is the most powerful animal when it's nervous and fearful?

DAY 333

What other hobbies or interests do you have?

DAY 334

List of things that you are letting go of

DAY 335

In hindsight, would you do it differently?

DAY 336

What should you not do at night, if you're not going to sleep?

DAY 337

List of things that are clearly and unequivocally wrong

DAY 338

If you could start today what would you start?

DAY 339

What else should you know before you go?

DAY 340

If you could have the same, who would it be?

DAY 341

How would you describe the feeling of being under scrutiny?

DAY 342

If you had a choice between two superpowers what would you get?

DAY 343

Describe a time when you were given a responsibility that you were not ready for.

DAY 344

Why do things have to stay as they are?

DAY 345

Why is it sometimes hard to forgive others?

DAY 346

If you had to choose one thing you could change to improve your career chances, what would it be?

DAY 347

What is the worst thing you've done in your life?

DAY 348

If you had to choose one film soundtrack to listen to, what would it be and why?

DAY 349

What's the best memory you have from the last year?

DAY 350

How would you describe the feeling of being incompetent?

DAY 351

Should you keep it a secret?

DAY 352

What is one thing you have in common with your son?

DAY 353

What is the worst thing you've done that will affect you?

DAY 354

What kind of art is your favorite? Why?

DAY 355

Who is the person that you feel has altered the course of your morals and values and how did they affect you?

DAY 356

How can women/men be happy with the way men/women look and feel, but still be attracted to them?

DAY 357

Would you rather fight a pack of hungry wolves or a pack of hungry monkeys?

DAY 358

Why, when, where and how is this happening now in your life

DAY 359

List of things to save time

DAY 360

What has made you feel that you have learned the truth that there is much more to life than just what you have been taught?

DAY 361

What is one thing that has changed about the world?

DAY 362

Did I do something today that I can be proud of? What was it?

DAY 363

What would you not feel if your father is gay?

DAY 364

What is the worst thing you've ever gotten paid for?

DAY 365

What would you do if you won the lottery and lose it the next day?

DAY 366

What do you do to help you create a unique experience?

www.ingramcontent.com/pod-product-compliance
Lightning Source LLC
Chambersburg PA
CBHW050803080726
47818CB00039B/421

9781989921111